Jacqueline Morley studied English at Oxford University. She has taught English and History and has a special interest in the history of everyday life. She is the author of several historical non-fiction books for children including **Clothes** in the *Timelines* series and the prize-winning **An Egyptian Pyramid** in the *Inside Story* series.

Illustrated by: Pam Hewetson
                   Nick Hewetson
                   Dave Antram
                   Gerald Wood

David Salariya was born in Dundee, Scotland. He has designed and created the award-winning *Timelines*, *New View*, *X-Ray Picture Book* and *Inside Story* series and many other books for publishers in the UK and abroad. He lives in Brighton with his wife, the illustrator Shirley Willis, and their son Jonathan.

Editor: Karen Barker Smith

© The Salariya Book Company Ltd
MCMXCIX

Created, designed and produced by

THE SALARIYA BOOK COMPANY LTD
25 Marlborough Place, Brighton BN1 1UB

ISBN 0 7500 2729 0

Published in 1999 by
MACDONALD YOUNG BOOKS
an imprint of Wayland Publishers Ltd
61 Western Road
Hove BN3 1JD

You can find Macdonald Young Books on the internet at http://www.myb.co.uk

A CIP catalogue record for this book is available from the British Library.

Printed in Hong Kong.

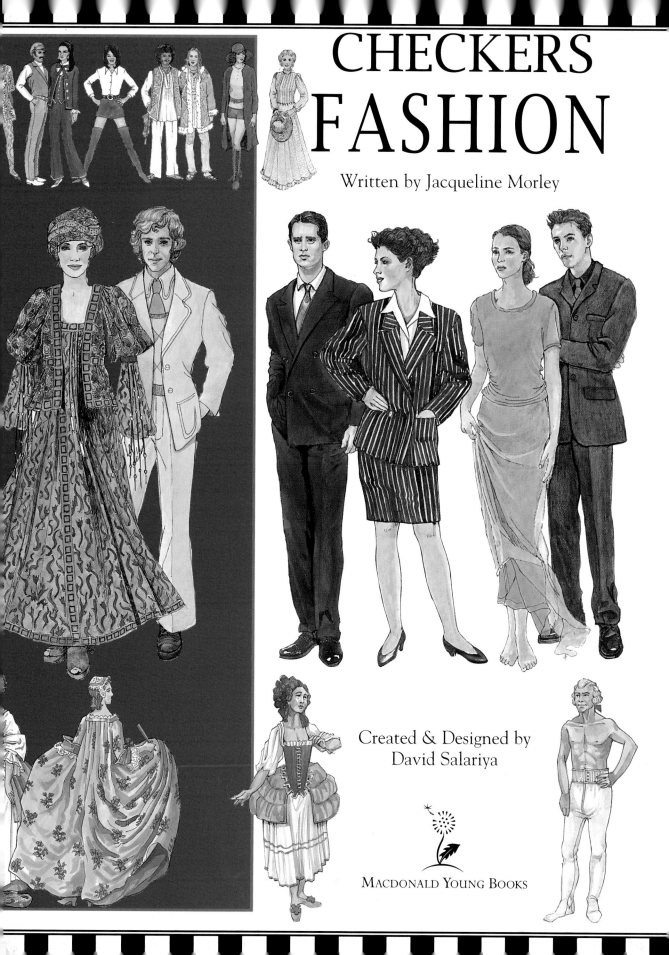

CHECKERS
FASHION

Written by Jacqueline Morley

Created & Designed by
David Salariya

MACDONALD YOUNG BOOKS

Contents

The ancient world

Fashion has been around for a long time. Archaeologists have found the remains of animal skin garments from 23,000 years ago decorated with shells and beads. This suggests that the urge to make clothes for more reason than just keeping warm is basic to human nature. The first sewn garments were made of stitched skins and later, of woven cloth. The earliest fashions which are known with any certainty are those of Mesopotamia and ancient Egypt, at about 3000 BC. The rulers of these great civilisations wore the finest cloth and jewellery to reflect their power and to impress their subjects.

Palaeolithic (Old Stone Age) family, c. 21,000 BC, wearing skins decorated with seashells, ivory beads and animal teeth.

Early Mesopotamian priest and queen (above). His tufted skirt copies earlier garments made of skins. The queen wears a magnificent gold wreath.

Crook and flail (royal emblems)

False beard

Royal head-dresses

Wig of human hair

Jewelled and enamelled collar

Transparent overtunic

Narrow sheath

Gold armband

This Egyptian pharaoh and his queen, about 1300 BC, wear head-dresses and jewellery that proclaim them to be gods on Earth, for that is what the Egyptians believed their kings to be.

Long pleated loincloth

Toe-strap sandals

Factfile: Egyptians
• White linen was in fashion for 3000 years. Men wore it as loincloths, women as narrow sheath dresses. Rich people added an overtunic of expensive transparent linen.
• Men and women wore wigs, perfume and heavy eye make-up.
• Workers often went naked.

Woollen headband

Tunic (chiton)

Large cloak (himation)

Ancient Greek gold necklace and ring. The finest Greek goldsmith's work was delicate. The Romans preferred chunky jewellery.

Thonged sandals

The ancient Greeks wore tunics made of rectangles of draped cloth, fastened with a brooch on the shoulders and often open at the side. For warmth they added a cloak made of another large rectangle of cloth. Men might wear the cloak alone, without a tunic, leaving a shoulder bare. The earliest Greek clothes were woollen. The use of thin linen (a 6th century BC fashion influence from Asia Minor) brought wide, gathered tunics into favour. Roman dress was similar, though the typical male garment, a cloak known as a toga, was semicircular.

Ancient Greek couple (above). The woman has doubled her tunic over at the top before pinning and belting it. Its hem is embroidered.

Right, a typical Roman family. Roman women (and Greek ones also) covered their head with their cloak when outdoors.

Short tunic

Toga

Tunic girdled at hips and waist

Cloak (palla)

Beneath their tunics Greek and Roman people probably wore garments like these (above). These images were found in a Roman floor mosaic.

7

The dark ages

When 5th century barbarian invaders conquered Rome, its traditions of luxurious living survived at Byzantium (in modern Turkey). Byzantium was the capital of the surviving eastern half of Rome's former empire and controlled the trade from China, Persia and India in silks, spices and gems, making it immensely rich. Its emperor and courtiers lived in the greatest magnificence. Eastern splendour was reflected in their clothes of stiff, jewel-encrusted silks.

The man and woman below (right) are in the type of clothes worn, with little variation, by the Anglo-Saxons (in England) and the Franks (in France) from the 7th to the 11th centuries. Both wear tunics (the woman's is called a gown) over narrow-wristed undertunics. The woman's cloak is a circle of fabric put on over the head. She wears a kerchief – a cloth covering her head – as women did in public. Nobles' clothes were made of better cloth with more ornament.

Tablion, a decorative panel denoting rank

Jewelled diadem

Ropes of pearls

Jewelled collar

Kerchief

Semi-circular cloak

Circular cloak

Silk tunic

Silk cloak

Shoes with ankle decorations

Undertunic

Braies

Overgown

Embroidery of gold thread, set with emeralds

Above left, a 6th century Byzantine emperor and empress in gold-embroidered silk tunics and large semi-circular cloaks, which replaced togas.

7th century Frankish brooch (left) and buckle (far left) of 'cloisonne', made by filling compartments with coloured enamel. The method came from the near east, via Byzantium.

Factfile: Byzantine
• Until the 6th century, silk had to be imported from China, for only the Chinese knew how to make it. Then (according to legend), two missionary monks sent by the Byzantine empress smuggled silkworms out of China hidden in a hollow cane. Byzantium was then able to start its own silk production.
• Precious stones, pearls and shimmering gold thread were used as decorations.
• The richest weaves and costliest dyes were reserved for the emperor's family.

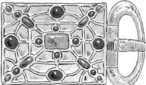

Meanwhile, in war-torn Europe merchants feared travelling, so luxuries were scarce. Most people wore homespun wool and never thought of fashion. Yet some notion of Byzantine styles trickled through and, as conditions improved, rulers tried to copy them. The 9th century Frankish ruler Charlemagne was buried in his ceremonial robes – tunics of the richest Byzantine silk, one set with rubies. For everyday wear he preferred traditional northern dress – a knee-length tunic and braies (long breeches, bound at the lower leg).

Viking bead necklace, hung with trinkets

Cloak brooch

Dress brooch

10th-century Viking in their version of the north European tunic, cloak and braies (below left).

Animal-skin cloak

Open gown

Bound braies

Loose braies

Deep decorative border

Gown

Below: Viking ribbon for garment edging. It could be woven in complicated patterns.

One Viking wears his braies loose (middle). His wife has a sideless top-gown held by brooches.

Factfile: Vikings
• Rich Vikings wore large gold collars and brooches to show off their wealth.
• Warlords rewarded their followers after battle by giving them heavy gold neck rings and arm bands.
• Vikings were enterprising merchants, going on long and dangerous journeys to foreign markets in search of goods to sell. They even brought back Byzantine silks for the few Vikings who could afford them.

Viking women hung toiletry implements (ear and nail cleaners) from a brooch at their chest.

Medieval times

A 12th-century queen and nobleman. Both wear a wide-sleeved overtunic or overgown. The queen's is mostly hidden by her cloak.

Variations on the tunic, overtunic and cloak continued to be worn throughout Europe in the 11th, 12th and 13th centuries. Nobles wore fine versions and peasants had hard-wearing ones. Tunics, even men's, trailed about the feet and had side or back-lacing which shaped them to the chest. Sleeves were enormously wide at the wrist. The simpler 13th-century styles, widening to the hem, often had sleeveless overtunics. In the 14th century, men's tunics were much shorter and body hugging. By 1350 they barely covered the hips and were worn with a low belt.

Kerchief

Undergown

Overtunic

Medieval undergarments: Men's hose are in separate legs and are only attached at the top. Women wore a simple undergown.

Factfile: Medieval
• Knights returning from the Crusades brought back a taste for luxury – rich weaves, silks and furs.
• The points of men's shoes were so long by the end of the 14th century that they had to be fastened to their knees by chains.

Sleeves of overgown

Plaits with false hair added

1150   1170   1240   1250   1280   1317

1150: Side lacing and cuffs so long they have to be knotted. 1170: Three-quarter length fur overtunic.

1240: The children wear typical 13th-century gowns – narrow-wristed, flaring and often unbelted.

1250: A new type of top garment with slits for the arms. It was fashionable to let its sleeves hang empty.

1280: Married women still covered their heads and sometimes wore a wimple – a cloth from neck to chin.

1317: The man's hooded and dagged overgown is open from shoulder to hem; the woman's has deep cut-away armholes.

A wealthy man and his wife, about 1240. He wears a full cloak, narrow-wristed, calf-length tunic and undertunic.

Her flat cap, hairnet and linen chin band are typical of the time. So is the cord holding her cloak.

The couple below are from about 1380. The woman's scooped neck and figure-hugging, tightly buttoned overgown are typically 14th century. The cuffs of the overgown sleeves end in long streamers of cloth, known as tippets.

The man is wearing a houppelande, a garment that replaced the cloak. It was often ankle length.

Fur cap

Linen coif (underbonnet)

Fur collar

Linen band (barbette)

Face-framing plaits

Undergown sleeves

Tippet

'Dagged' (slit) edges

Buttoned sleeves

Brooch closing undergown

Hanging purse

Slit for access to hanging purse beneath

Long-pointed shoes

Front slit for ease of riding a horse

1330

1359

1365

1380

1395

1330: Noble woman with a long ceremonial train and a wimple. The sides of her overgown are laced.

1359: Nobleman in the new, short tunic. His wife's overgown is so cut away that the front is just a strip.

1365: Fashionable man in a short cape; girl in a striped overgown with elbow-length sleeves and tippets.

1380: Man in a cape and patterned houppelande. The cuffs of his undergown cover his hands.

1395: Women wore houppelandes too. This has immensely wide sleeves. and her head-dress is dagged to match.

15th century

Burgundian enamelled hat brooch with a cameo portrait. Men wore large brooches on their hats and women wore them in their hair.

Factfile: Late Medieval styles
• Some men wore parti-coloured garments and hose (the left side different from the right).
• Footwear went to new lengths, with points stiffened with whalebone and pattens (separate wooden soles).
• Sleeves came in all shapes: from empty, trailing ones to those with stuffed shoulders or sleeves made of small pieces joined up with lacing.

y the 15th century, fashion was not just for kings, queens and the nobility. Trade increased throughout the middle ages and by now some merchant families were so rich that they lent money to kings. Such wealthy people could afford the best furs and richest silks, and those who were a little less rich did their best to copy them. The authorities often passed laws to try to stop them doing so – if everyone who could afford it was allowed to wear fine things, how could people identify the real nobles? As well as nobles in castles and peasants working the land there were now many comfortably-off people living in towns, who liked to show their prosperity by being seen in expensive clothes. Styles changed faster as people competed with each other and trends were taken to extremes. Women's headgear grew fantastically wide or tall, and young men wore extremely short garments with padded shoulders and sleeves. Regional differences became more pronounced. It was easy to tell an Italian from a Burgundian, for example, from the way they dressed. The rich Duchy of Burgundy set the fashions for northern Europe.

1416 French courtiers: The man's houppelande has fur-lined sleeves, patterned with crowns.

The woman's arms emerge from slits in her trailing sleeves which hang empty.

1430 Italians: The man has bag sleeves, tight at the wrists, while the woman's hair is dressed over a frame.

1448: Men's gowns are shorter and tightly belted to form neat folds. Pattens support the long-toed hose.

1450: The height of Burgundian fashion! A 'steeple' head-dress with a veil held out over a wire frame.

Mid 15th-century couple (below). The woman is wearing a high-waisted, broad-belted gown.

Her hair, dressed in a net on each side of her head, is topped with a padded roll.

The folds of the man's short overgown are padded and stitched to keep their shape.

The flap of cloth that hides the gap between the separate legs is called a codpiece.

To stop the braies showing under the very short top garments, the legs of the hose were tied to the bottom of the doublet with a codpiece in-between. Sleeves were separate and tied too.

Padded chest

Heart-shaped head-dress

Hat with trailing end wound around neck

Fur collar

Padded sleeves

Factfile: Renaissance

By the close of the 15th century, medieval ways of dressing had mostly vanished.
• Floating veils, pointed shoes, big head-dresses and long trains disappeared.
• Men's long gowns were quite out of fashion, except for old or pompous people.
• Instead of falling in folds, men's clothes were boxy with square shoulders.

Undergown

V-necked gown

1495

1495: Three young Venetians. Italian women did not wear the elaborate headgear of northern Europe. All three wear the new fashion for showing the shirt or chemise through gaps between the sleeve pieces. The man on the right wears an extremely short doublet and no overgown. Older people thought this was shocking.

16th century

The flowing tunics of medieval times were now a thing of the past. The 16th-century fashion demanded a stiff, almost sculpted look, and the clothes could almost stand up by themselves. This was partly due to the richly patterned brocades and heavy velvets which were used, and partly because garments were stiffened and padded in ways that had nothing to do with the human shape. Bombast (a stuffing of horsehair and rags) produced men's shoulders of enormous width; later in the century it gave them pumpkin-shaped thighs and padded bellies tapering to a point. Women's chests and stomachs were completely flattened by rigid corsets reinforced with strips of metal or whalebone.

Merman pendant. His body is made of a huge pearl.

1514 German couple (right). The man's garments are 'slashed' (slit to show the cloth below). This was a fashion fad that lasted, in less extreme forms, throughout the century.

Legwear was now formed of upper and lower hose. This man's upper hose cover the knee, but during the century they got shorter and wider and were often stuffed. In this form they were called trunk hose.

Plumed cap

Gold chains

Slashed doublet

Bodice collar

Sleeve in several pieces

The woman wears a gown of heavy silk, boldly patterned in bands. Its bodice opening is laced across. Later in the century, this area was filled by a stomacher – a rigid fabric-covered triangle. The man's shirt forms a decorative frill at his neck. During the century this grew larger and stiffer and developed into the ruff.

Slashed overgown

Upper hose

Lower hose

Long girdle

Blunt-toed shoes

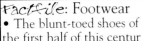

Factfile: Footwear
• The blunt-toed shoes of the first half of this century were padded to seem as broad as they were long.
• Hose were now made of knitted wool instead of cloth, which gave a much better fit.

Henry VIII
1536

Flat cap

Wide fur collar

Slashed doublet

Codpiece

Fur-lined
overgown

Jerkin
with deep
U-neck

The 1530s
cube look: the
flat cap, padded
doublet and wide-
collared overgown
with bulging
sleeves form a
totally square figure.

Above, the Spanish
farthingale and, below,
the French farthingale,
a variation that appeared
in the late 1570s.

Queen Elizabeth I, 1592

Ruff
supported
by wire
frame

Ruff of
starched
lace

Stomacher

Jewel-encrusted
brocade over
French
farthingale

1546

1550

1555

1560

1571

1581

1588

1595

1546: Skirted
doublet and overgown.
1550: Farthingale
under open skirt and
cushion-sleeved
overgown.

1555: Short Spanish
cloak. 1560: Softer
Italian woman's
gown and men's
short jerkin, doublet
and hose.

1571: High Spanish
ruff encircling neck,
open sleeve caught
at wrist, skirt closed
with ribbon ties.

1581: Open ruff and
French
farthingale; cape
and brief trunk hose
with canions (upper
leg coverings).

1588: Wide ruff,
belly-padded
doublet. 1595:
Stuffed trunk hose;
boy in soft collar
and breeches.

17th century

1630: High waisted, long-skirted doublet, cloak and breeches in slashed and braided satin. The plumed hat, riding boots and lavish use of lace are typical of the time.

Wide-brimmed hat

Long curls

Lace cuffs

Wide-topped boots with lace trimmed linings

Early in the century the stiff Spanish style gave way to a softer look. Ruffs became drooping collars and stiff brocades were replaced by lightweight silks and lace. Women's gowns were wide-shouldered and full-sleeved with gathered skirts of billowing silk. After 1670 the female silhouette was narrower and stiffer. Men added lavish flounces of lace at the neck, wrists and knees. In the 1660s, they were wearing 'petticoat' breeches with trims of looped ribbon and legs so wide they looked like a skirt. This was too outrageous to last long. In the 1670s a new garment, the 'vest', a simple, narrow-sleeved, front-buttoning jacket, appeared. With narrow breeches and a coat, it formed the earliest three-piece suit.

1636

Lace-trimmed collar

1636: The sloping shape of the collar is continued by the swelling sleeves. The bodice is seamed to fit snugly. It was fashionable to show some underskirt.

1618

1634

1640

1645

1646

1618: Stiff open ruff, short-skirted doublet, baggy breeches and shoes with large rosettes.

1634: The man's hair is longer, his breeches tighter and his collar and boots are draped in lace.

1640: Loose-ended breeches, decorated at the hem, meet boots with 'bucket' tops.

1645: Side ringlets, high waist, almost off-the-shoulder neckline, and skirt drawn up to show underskirt.

1646: Short doublet showing shirt bloused out over ribbon-trimmed breeches, boot tops filled with lace.

Court lady of 1690

Necklines are no longer wide and slipping off the shoulders. Instead, the fashionable look is narrow-shouldered, with the chest squashed up towards the chin with firm corseting.

Fontange

Beauty patch

Narrow, three-quarter sleeves

Muff

Falls of lace

Tiered underskirt

Overskirt

Above, a pendant of ivory, enamel and gold, in the form of a 'momento mori' (a reminder of death). Repeated plagues and wars meant death was frequently encountered. Skulls and coffins were common motifs in jewellery.

The head-dress of wired lace, attached to a linen cap, was called a fontange. It was typical of the 1690s.

'Patches' – small dots of black velvet or silk stuck to the face – were thought to be attractive.

The deeply-frilled velvet overskirt matches the bodice. The skirt is looped back to show its decorative lining and arranged to form a bustle and short train.

The skirt and underskirt are still made separately from the bodice. Underskirts are no longer meant to be hidden. They are made in expensive materials and have become an important part of the gown. This one is made in three deep flounces.

> **Factfile: 17th century**
> • High heels began to be worn and by the end of the century they were frequently over 8cm high.
> • Fashionable hair was long. Both sexes favoured wearing wigs rather than caring for all that hair.

1660 **1663** **1674** **1678** **1683** **1693**

1660: 'Petticoat' breeches.
1663: Longer hair, more ribbon and flounces at the knee.

1674: Necklines are higher and narrower, trimmings more elaborate, ornamental aprons are in fashion.

1678: Return to simpler fashion – a long-sleeved, fitted coat worn with a wide-brimmed hat for men.

1683: Buttoned coat and winter greatcoat. The brim of the hat is 'cocked' (bent up).

1693: Women's hunting clothes in male style. A couple in walking clothes – both carry muffs.

18th century

A wealthy English woman of 1715 in riding clothes. Her cocked hat, cravat and full-skirted coat with wide buttoned-back cuffs copy the latest fashions for men.

Cocked hat

Man's cravat

Pockets buttoned to match cuffs

Women now took the fashion lead. Coats and breeches remained the rule for men, the coat becoming slimmer as the century progressed. Meanwhile, women varied their shape amazingly. At first, skirts swelled out over underskirts reinforced with hoops. The width then moved to the sides, supported by 'panniers' (the French word for baskets) which were cane constructions worn over the hips. In the 1770s women pulled their hair up over tall pads or wire frames and topped them with fantastic decorations. By the 1780s broad hats exaggerated the width of womens' heads and the most fashionable women wore a plain white dress like a chemise (a sleeved petticoat), sashed at the waist.

> **Factfile: 18th century**
> • By the 1740s, fashionable skirts were so wide (up to 4 metres across) that women had to turn sideways to get through doors.
> • Men of the upper classes, who used to carry swords, now carried canes instead. But the custom of buttoning the coat from left to right (originally to let the right hand slip in easily to draw the sword) was by now standard practice. It is the same today.

Diamond brooch in the form of a bow, for the top of a stomacher.

1707: Frills are in fashion; frilled muslin cap and deep, stiff flounces on the skirt and underskirt.

1726: The coat of the early part of the century, nipped at the waist, with deep cuffs and a stiffened skirt.

1731: 'Sack' gown of embroidered silk, falling in a train of loose pleats from the shoulders.

1744: A humbler style; the customary low neckline is filled in by a fichu – a square of fine white linen.

1749: Panniers at their widest; a lace cap is always worn, except on the grandest occasions.

Because of her skirt the mother rides side-saddle (breeches were unthinkable for women). Her jacket folds back to form revers.

Revers

The father (below) wears a country 'frock' coat. These had a turned down collar and narrow cuffs or none at all; their cut-away front was more convenient for riding.

Plain skirt

Round country hat

Short waistcoat

No cuffs

Trousers

Riding boots

Chemise dress

1770s underwear (above): chemise, long corset and small panniers.

1770s English family in the country (right). The parents wear clothes designed for riding. English aristocrats enjoyed the country and spent so much time there that it became smart for young men to be seen in country clothes, even in London. The fashion caught on abroad – by the 1780s elegant Frenchmen (no lovers of the countryside) were copying the English country style.

1790s drawers (above) with separate legs joined only to the waistband.

The little boy and his sister are wearing children's styles. Comfortable clothes for children were a new idea. Until this period they were dressed in smaller versions of adult fashions, including ruffs, corsets and sometimes even wigs.

1759

1770

1771

1777

1781

1786

1759: Narrower coat with a turn-down collar; full skirts but no exaggerated panniers for day wear.

1770: Court evening dress. Big panniers are no longer worn by day but formal styles are slow to change.

1771: Cut-away coat front showing the now shorter waistcoat. 1777: 'Polonaise' gown, gathered at the back.

1781: English smart casual wear for town – a plain wool riding coat, round-brimmed country hat and boots.

1786: A French 'redingote' (from 'riding coat') and muslin chemise gown, displaying the new simplicity.

Early 19th century

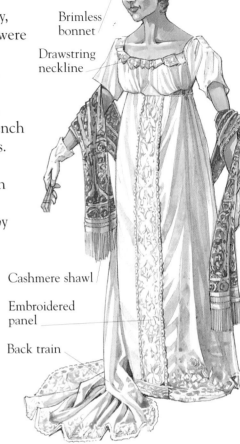

Brimless bonnet

Drawstring neckline

At the end of the 18th century, when freedom and equality were in the air, fashions became simple and less constricting. These ideals were taken to extremes during the French Revolution. While the revolution lasted, elegant French people dressed like workers and peasants. When order was restored, fashionable clothing returned. However, people soon forgot that the wearing of trousers had started out as a symbol of revolution – by 1820 they were standard wear for men.

1794: Clothes of the Revolution. Working class trousers and apron and a specially designed 'citizen's costume', which did not catch on.

Factfile: Politics and clothes
• During the Revolution people had to take care what they wore. Clothes or styles associated with the court, like panniers and powdered hair, aroused suspicions. The wearer could easily be condemned as a traitor and executed.
• Keen revolutionaries tried to show that they were men of the people by wearing trousers. Until then, these had only been worn by workers and children – gentlemen had worn breeches.

1806 evening dress of embroidered muslin (right). High-waisted, narrow-skirted garments had been in fashion since the end of the last century. White was the favoured colour and a long cashmere shawl was the favourite accessory.

Cashmere shawl

Embroidered panel

Back train

1798   1802   1808   1811   1814   1815

1798: French chemise with ribbon decoration based on the way aristocrats were tied for execution.

1802: Skimpy dresses, sometimes dampened to cling, were supposed to give the look of a Greek statue.

1808: Men now wore top hats and long tight breeches, or nearly skin-tight trousers known as pantaloons.

1811: Evening dress, still high-waisted, but much more vivid in colour and decoration than before.

1814: Lady's travelling coat worn with a small fur cape. 1815: Two young girls in walking clothes.

Top hat
(essential wear)

Silk
cravat

Wide-brimmed
bonnet

Wide collar
and revers

Broad lace collar

Gilt
buttons

Long tight cuffs

Pleated
bodice

Gathered
trouser
front

1828 men's
underwear (above):
muslin shirt with a
tucked front and a
high, stiffened collar
with points.

1828: The man is
wearing a formal 'tail'
coat, a descendant of
the country riding
coat. As often
happens, the sports
clothes of one period
have become formal
wear in the next. (A
version of this outfit is
still seen today at
smart weddings.)

1830 women's
underwear (above):
a tight-waisted, back-
laced corset over a
chemise with padded
sleeves.

1828 walking dress
of printed cotton.
The look is still
high-waisted but
the skirt is fuller
(held out by layers
of petticoats).
Bonnet, collar and
padded sleeves
emphasise the top
half of the body
while flounces at
the hem echo this.

1817   1823   1828   1829   1829   1830

1817: A walking
dress, its wider hem
embellished with
padded bands.
1823: hats are
wider, waists lower.

1828: Double-
breasted day coat
with 'leg-of-mutton'
sleeves, full at the
shoulder and tight
at the wrist.

1829: Emphatic
hats and hem
decorations were in
fashion. A wide
neckline sets off the
tiny waist.

1829: Single-
breasted greatcoat
with padded sleeves;
for evening wear, a
tailcoat and
pantaloons.

1830: Wide
shoulders taken to
extremes, with
balloon sleeves,
flounces and a
lower waistline.

Late 19th century

Below, an 1840s gold bracelet in the shape of a snake. Its enamelled head is set with diamonds.

Factfile: Hems and crinolines
• By the 1850s skirts could measure 10 metres around the hem, sometimes more if made of very thin silk or muslin.
• In 1856 a Frenchman patented the crinoline, a frame of flexible steel hoops, which replaced all the petticoats that had previously been needed under these skirts.

Trade boomed in the 19th century, creating a rich middle class which displayed its wealth by wearing expensive clothes. Men were expected to dress seriously for the serious job of making money, but their wives and daughters could be as gaudy as they liked. Fashion magazines started to appear, and from the 1850s women's fashions were incredibly extravagant in fabrics and trimmings. Poorly paid working women spent long hours hand sewing huge crinoline skirts and, later, bustles. The invention of the sewing machine did little to help them; it only increased the demand for trimmings. Critics who said corsets were unhealthy and bustles ridiculous went unheeded. Only the concept of sportswear, first appearing in the 1870s, made simpler styles acceptable.

Necklaces in the form of snakes were popular too. The snake went round the throat in the form of a chain and often had a heart-shaped locket hanging from its jaws.

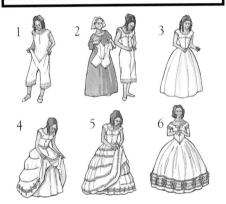

1840s underwear: 1) Chemise and drawers; 2) Then a tight waisted corset and a camisole; 3) Next a petticoat of stiff woven horsehair; 4) Then one reinforced with stitching; 5) Over this, two or more starched layers; 6) Finally a muslin one with a fancy hem.

1833: Winter outdoor gown of velvet with embroidered panels, worn with a muff, bonnet and veil.

1834: Men's day wear, tight-waisted, with sloping shoulders. 1836: Women's sleeves have gone droopy.

1837: Big sleeves are out, little bonnets are in. Mother and daughter both have skirts with lots of trimming.

1840: A new waistline, V-shaped in front. 1845: Huge shawls over wide skirts made women look triangular.

1847: Man in a high-buttoned waistcoat and shirt with standing collar. Woman with winter fur muff.

1866: Walking dress of striped silk, worn over a crinoline. The first crinolines were circular, producing a 'tea-cosy' skirt, but the rounded front was inconvenient and made it difficult to get near other people without tilting the frame up at the back. 1860s crinolines were much flatter in front but elongated behind, forming a train.

Fringed braid trim

The crinoline frame (below), made of flexible steel hoops, held petticoat and skirt well clear of the legs. The man wears a vest with open armpits.

The tiny brim-less bonnet is tied with an enormous bow beneath the chin.

Glass buttons

Slightly raised waist

The front buttoning bodice is separate from the skirt. Some skirts had two tops, one for day and one for evening wear.

Oversleeve

Narrow undersleeve

This dress has quite a small train by the standards of the 1860s. Some crinolines stuck out far behind their wearers.

Lace shawl

1871

1875

1877   1880

1880

1871: Skirts are held up in the small of the back by a horsehair or wire bustle. The man wears a loose jacket.

1875: Fur-lined coat with big collar and cuffs. The woman's dress has an open overskirt bunched up over a bustle.

1877: Evening dress, showing how much skirts have slimmed in ten years, with all the fullness at the back.

1880: Very tight skirts are briefly in fashion, but bustles were to make a come back in the mid 1890s.

1880: Clothes designed for sport; cap, jacket and knickerbockers for shooting; bathing dress; cycling gear.

1900-1929

Before the First World War fashionable clothes were elaborate and needed a lot of care and attention to be worn properly. However, women gained more independence and freedom during the war, and afterwards they wanted that to continue. Designers responded with shorter-skirted styles, very daring at the time. Less wealthy people could now buy fashionable styles too, thanks to the mass manufacture of machine-made clothes.

Lace-trimmed hat

'Choker' neckline

Straw boater

Double-breasted jacket

Stiff shirt collar

Long gloves

1905 woollen travelling dress

1904 flannel boating suit

Factfile: Pre-war
• Rich women had several changes of clothes per day: informal day wear, morning walking dress, tea gowns for receiving friends, afternoon dress for visiting, dinner gowns and full evening dress.

1910 underwear: Suspenders, attached to the bottom of the corset have replaced garters for holding up women's stockings.

1901   1905   1908   1910   1912   1913   1914   1918

1901: The turn of the century shape, made by the 'S-bend' corset, pinched in at the back.

1905: Motoring coat, worn with a flat cap. 1908: Waistless dress by rebel French designer, Paul Poiret.

1910: Poiret's slender look has caught on, worn with very wide hats, and here, with a long fur stole.

1912: A bridesmaid's dress with low V-neck. 1913: Wrap-over skirts allow for walking in ankle-tight styles.

1914: Overtunics are popular on dresses and as part of suits. 1918: A raincoat with raglan sleeves.

1925: Short silk evening dress, decorated with heavy embroidery of glass beads and imitation pearls. The embroidery design and the hanging girdle were inspired by ancient Egypt. The discovery of Tutankhamun's tomb in 1922 had a great impact on fashion.

Square neckline

Heavy beading

Bobbed hair

Long pearl necklace

White bow tie

The woman's partner wears full evening dress – a black tailcoat and trousers, a black, or more usually white, waistcoat, and a white bow tie. For less formal evenings a dinner jacket (without tails) could be worn, in which case the bow tie had to be black. These rules are still followed today.

Beaded girdle

Factfile: Post-war
• The 1920s ideal woman dressed to look waistless and bustless.
• At first, fashionable skirts were long, reaching the ankles in 1922, but hemlines rose to their shortest in 1926-27, but not above the knee.
• Women's hair was 'bobbed' (cut very short) and brimless 'cloche' hats were worn.

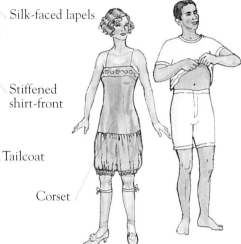

Silk-faced lapels

Stiffened shirt-front

Tailcoat

Corset

Only especially curvy women had to wear corsets in the 1920s (above), but there were new undergarments – the brassiere (because corsets no longer came up high enough to support the bust) and 'cami-knickers' (combined camisole and knickers).

1921   1922   1922   1925   1926   1928   1929

1921: A 'coat dress' – a front-buttoning garment designed to look like a two piece, with a fox fur stole.

1922: Men in smart town clothes with bowler hats. The woman wears a long day dress and the girl has a cloche hat.

1925: A low back is popular for evening. The hair is boyish but the gauzy floating panels are feminine.

1926: The shortest skirts yet. 1928: Cutting fabric on the bias makes clothes cling to the body.

1929: longer daytime skirts – a day dress of spotted silk and a two-piece trimmed with monkey fur.

1930-1959

B y the thirties, ordinary people were becoming much more fashion conscious. Despite widespread unemployment, those in work had more spending power than in the past. Popular magazines, advertising and the cinema were all great fashion influences. The new 'casual' clothes appeared: shorts, 'slacks' and backless tops, as more people took up weekend activities and sunbathing became the new health craze. During the Second World War, all goods were in short supply and clothes had to be skimpy. 'Make do and mend' was the slogan. No wonder that the 1947 'New Look', which required huge amounts of cloth for long, full skirts, was a fashion sensation.

1930s underwear (above): Lightweight elasticated corset, Y-front pants invented in 1934.

Factfile: The Thirties
• The thirties look was long and slender, with calf-length skirts.
• Trousers for women were now acceptable as sportswear, or for informal evenings when they were wide and looked like skirts.

Drooping skirts, drooping sleeves, long gloves and little tilted hats created the mid-thirties 'lady-like' look.

Permed hair

Hat with veil

Gathered sleeves

Gloves, still essential

Court shoes

Fur stole

1931   1932   1933   1933   1936   1943

1943

1931: Beach pyjamas for summer relaxation.

1933: Younger women like sportswear with a masculine cut.

1933: Couple in evening dress. A dinner jacket is now acceptable for all but the most formal evening events.

1936: Double-breasted travelling coats. All the family wear hats and the children have leggings for warmth.

1943: A draped dress, square-cut jacket and coat, all with boxy shoulders created with large shoulder pads.

1940s woollen suit

Fair Isle pullover

Brylcreem in hair

Boxer shorts

Sock suspenders

Trilby hat

Matching jacket and trousers (known as a lounge suit, left) was now the usual daytime wear. Checked tweed and knitted pullover (in place of a waistcoat) give this outfit an informal air.

1947: 'New Look' dress in plain black, which focuses attention on the new silhouette. A huge bow emphasises the scooped neck.

Off-the-shoulder collar

Nipped-in waist

Long gloves

Ankle-strap shoes

In 1947 French designer Christian Dior showed a collection of clothes that became immediately famous as 'The New Look'. After the shortages of the Second World War, women were thrilled by his lavish use of material and totally new shape – rounded shoulders, tiny waists and long, full skirts.

Stiff petticoats were needed under the full-skirts of the 50s. Also a strapless bra for evening wear.

Ballerina length full skirt

Factfile: Forties and Fifties
• The 40s began with shorter skirts, padded shoulders and square toes. They ended with swaying, full skirts, or very narrow ones with a 'kick-pleat' to make walking possible.
• 50s styles were tight-waisted and big-busted until the 1958 waistless 'sack' dress appeared.

1946   1947   1948   1948   1953   1955   1959
                                                    1954

1946: 'Swagger' coat falling straight from the shoulders. 1947: 'New Look' suit with swinging skirt.

1948: Dior suit with long narrow skirt, 'fly-away' cuffs and jacket stiffened to stand out at the hips.

1948: Couple in formal evening wear. 1953: Figure-hugging suit emphasises rounded hips.

1954: Full-skirted summer dress in flowered cotton. 1955: A-line skirt and jacket, widening towards the hem.

1959: Pixie hats and rompers for children, shorter hemlines for adults. Even men's overcoats are shorter.

1960s to 1990s

Raised hairstyle

Heavy eye make-up

Tight armholes

Above knee hemline

Young people were earning more than ever before in the 60s and they had more money available to spend on fashion. Even after the Second World War fashion meant clothes for women who wanted to look 25. Since teenagers became such important buyers of fashion in the 60s, designers and manufacturers have looked to the youthful worlds of sport, pop music and street fashion for inspiration. Trousers, T-shirts and trainers are now part of everyone's wardrobe. It is not the design but the designer label that makes a difference.

Factfile:
Sixties and Seventies
• In the 60s, the majority of women wore miniskirts. Like the 1850s crinoline, it was a skirt style that was accepted by everybody.
• However the miniskirt went out of favour quickly. In the winter of 67-68 smart hems were suddenly at the ankles.

1968: Double-breasted suit of striped corduroy, by English designer Mr Fish. Dazzling 'psychedelic' colours were popular.

Bright boots

1965: Silk mini-dress by French designer Ives St. Laurent (left). Its 'window pane' design was inspired by modern abstract painting. The dress was a success and was immediately copied by manufacturers who mass-produced cheaply for high street shops.

From the 60s onwards, cheap copies of designer clothes quickly made their way to high street stores.

1961: Armpit hugging 'Jackie Kennedy' suit. 1962: Pant-suit – drainpipe trousers and matching top.

1965: Street fashion – A 'Mod' in cap, hipster pants and turtle neck. 1966: Velvet trouser suit for evenings.

1967: The 60s miniskirt at its shortest. Boots, the essential footwear, go thigh-high to meet it.

1970: Hippies reject commercial styles for peasant clothes, beads, caftans and Afghan leather coats.

1972: For a short while 'hot pants' replace skirts, even for work. 1975: Romantic cotton maxi-dress.

70s hippy-inspired dress by Bill Gibb; suit with wide lapels, patch pockets and flared trousers.

80s 'yuppies', dressed to look like city bankers.

90s simple T-shirt and skirt in see-through fabric. The man wears a dark suit appropriate for work or formal occasions.

Turban hat

Small collar

Kipper tie

Shoulder pads

Narrow tie

Dark shirt and tie

Tank top

Flared trousers

Flaring ankle-length skirt

Thin jersey fabric

Platform shoes

Slimline trousers

Turn-ups

'Office' suit

1977

1983

1984

1986

1993

1995

1998

1994

1977: Punk street fashion, 'Mohican' hair, metal-studded, black leather jackets, fishnet tights.

1983: Power dressing for business women – maxi-coat, trouser suit, shirt and tie.

1984: Family in waterproof casuals.
1986: Simple clothes, fancy price, by Italian designer Giorgio Armani.

1993: Baseball cap, T-shirt and jogging bottoms, jeans. Man in the 'linen look' – designer suit, no tie.

1994: Sheath dress. 1995: Strappy shift dress.1998: Combat trousers (for both sexes) and bare midriff.

Fashion Quiz

1. Who were the only people not allowed to wear a toga?
a) Roman emperors
b) Roman citizens
c) Roman slave

2. What were braies?
a) A type of men's breeches
b) Medieval plaits
c) 19th century dress trimming

3. In medieval times, what did 'dagging' a garment mean?
a) Dyeing it two different colours
b) Lining it
c) Cutting slits into the hems

4. What was whalebone used as a stiffener for?
a) Conical head-dresses
b) Men's trousers
c) The points of shoes

5. Where did women wear a fontange?
a) On their head
b) Round their neck
c) Round their waist

6. The 'New Look' fashions became popular after which period?
a) The French Revolution
b) The First World War
c) The Second World War

7. What was a houppelande?
a) A late medieval outer garment
b) An 18th century decorative underskirt
c) The French name for a crinoline

8. Who wore petticoat breeches?
a) Small boys in the 13th century
b) Men in the 17th century
c) Old ladies in the 19th century

9. Why did women wear a farthingale?
a) To hold up their ruffs
b) To hold out their skirts
c) To keep their shoes dry

10. What was a wimple?
a) A widow's cap
b) A decorative apron
c) A throat covering

Quiz answers are on page 32.

Glossary

bias
A way of cutting fabric so that the threads of its weave will hang diagonally when worn. Normally they hang vertically and horizontally.

boater
A flat-crowned, stiff-brimmed straw hat, originally worn for boating.

bowler hat A hard hat with a domed crown and a narrow curled brim.

Brylcreem A men's brand of hair-cream which gives hair a sleek, shiny look.

Burgundy A rich independent state in the Middle Ages. Now part of eastern central France.

cameo A precious stone or shell with two coloured layers. The top layer is partly cutaway to create a design contrasting with the different colour beneath.

camisole A woman's undergarment.

cashmere Costly Indian fabric made from the wool of the Cashmere goats of the western Himalayas.

choker A high neckline or necklace.

cocked hat Hat with the brim folded against the crown in three places, giving it a triangular shape.

coif Medieval close-fitting cap tied under the chin, worn by men and women, often under other headgear.

cravat A piece of lace, linen or silk tied around the neck.

doublet A man's short, front-opening overgarment, sometimes padded. It was worn from the 14th to the 17th centuries.

drawers
Undergarment for the lower part of the body and the upper legs. Originally it was formed of two pieces drawn up over each leg.

enamelled
Decorated with melted glass of various colours.

Franks A germanic people whose power extended over much of modern Germany and France from the 5th to the 9th century.

hippies
Followers of a 1960s Californian lifestyle which rejected material values in favour of a loving, sharing and relaxed attitude.

hot pants Very short shorts, briefly in fashion in the 1970s as a substitute for skirts.

kerchief A piece of cloth covering the head.

kipper tie A very wide tie worn in the 1970s.

loincloth Male garment formed by tying a piece of cloth around the hips.

Mesopotamia
A region of the ancient world, roughly equivalent to modern Iraq.

muslin Very fine, semi-transparent cotton fabric.

power dressing
An 1980s expression for a style of business clothes that suggest the wearer is high-powered at work.

raglan sleeve Sleeve with a top extending to the neckline.

revers The top part of the front opening of a jacket, folded back to show the underside.

sideburns Facial hair allowed to grow down the sides of the cheeks.

slacks Casual trousers.

stomacher
A triangle of stiffened and decorated material placed between or over the front edges of a bodice.

trilby Soft felt hat with a crease in the crown from back to front.

whalebone A horny substance from the upper jaw of a whale. Used as a stiffener in women's corsets until the invention of plastic replaced it.

yuppies A 1980s term created from the initials Y, U and P (young, upwardly-mobile persons). Used to describe pushy, newly successful people with plenty of disposable cash (money to spend).

Index

Quiz answers

1) c see page 7
2) a see page 9
3) c see page 11
4) c see page 12
5) a see page 17
6) c see page 26
7) a see page 11
8) b see page 16
9) b see pages 15
10) c see page 10

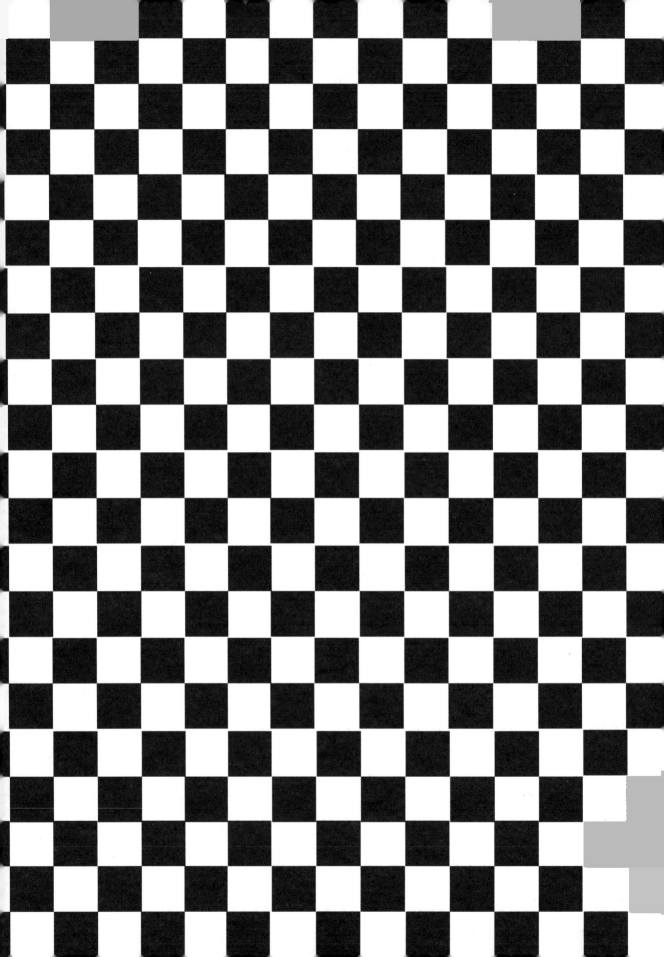